Unlocking Your True Self

Embark on the Ultimate Journey of Self-Discovery!

Peter H. Christian

Contents

CHAPTER 1

The Quest Within

How Well Do You Know Yourself?

In the vast expanse of existence, there is an uncharted realm—a journey that transcends the boundaries of the known. This is not a physical journey but a profound odyssey within, a quest to unravel the intricacies of your being. The question that echoes through the corridors of self-discovery is simple yet profound: How well do you know yourself?

Unveiling the Layers:

The human psyche is a labyrinth of thoughts, emotions, and experiences. To embark on the journey of self-discovery is to peel back the layers, exposing the core of your identity. It requires a willingness to explore the recesses of your mind, confront the shadows that linger, and embrace the light that emanates from within.

Reflective Exercise: Mapping Your Inner Landscape

Start your journey by creating a map of your inner landscape. Consider it a cartography of the self, marking significant milestones, experiences, and emotions. Identify the peaks of joy, the valleys of challenges, and the unexplored territories that beckon your curiosity. This exercise lays the foundation for a deeper understanding of your own terrain.

The Mirror of Reflection:

Self-discovery is akin to standing before a mirror—a mirror that reflects not just your physical form but the essence of who you are. It is a mirror that captures the nuances of your character, the tapestry of your beliefs, and the kaleidoscope of your aspirations. Gaze into this mirror with honesty and openness, for it is through reflection that the contours of your true self emerge.

Journaling Your Reflections

Take up the practice of reflective journaling. Dedicate time to articulate your thoughts, feelings, and observations about yourself. Use this as a tool to track your evolving understanding of who you are. Allow the journal to be a sanctuary for your unfiltered thoughts, a canvas on which you paint the portrait of your innermost self.

The Influence of Experiences:

Your journey of self-discovery is intertwined with the tapestry of your experiences. Every encounter, whether harmonious or discordant, leaves an imprint on the canvas of your identity. To know yourself is to acknowledge the impact of these experiences and discern the threads that weave through the fabric of your being.

Crafting Your Narrative

Consider your life as a story waiting to be written. Reflect on the pivotal chapters that have defined you — the triumphs that brought elation, the challenges that sculpted resilience, and the moments of vulnerability that revealed your authentic self. In understanding your narrative, you gain insight into the forces that have shaped you.

The Dance of Passions:

At the heart of self-discovery lies the recognition of your passions. What stirs your soul? What pursuits ignite the flames of enthusiasm within you? To know yourself is to identify and embrace your passions, for they are the compass that points toward your true north.

Passion-Exploration Exercise

Engage in activities that evoke passion within you. Whether it's a hobby, a form of art, or a cause that resonates, immerse yourself. Observe how these pursuits make you feel and what they unveil about your authentic desires. Your passions are gateways to self-revelation.

The Power of Introspection:

In the hustle of daily life, introspection becomes a beacon, guiding you back to the essence of self-awareness. Take moments of solitude to delve into the recesses of your thoughts. Introspection is not merely a retrospective gaze but a contemplative practice that unveils the present moment of your evolving self.

Introspective Meditation

Incorporate meditation into your routine, focusing on the present moment. Allow your thoughts to surface and observe them without judgment. This practice cultivates mindfulness, fostering a deep connection with your inner self.

Embracing Vulnerability:

To know yourself is to embrace vulnerability—the raw and unfiltered aspects of your being. It is an acknowledgment that perfection is an illusion, and authenticity resides in the acceptance of both strengths and vulnerabilities. Through vulnerability, you forge a profound connection with your true self.

Vulnerability Journaling

Create a "Vulnerability Journal" where you candidly explore moments of vulnerability. Reflect on how these moments shape your relationships, choices, and self-perception. Embracing vulnerability becomes a transformative act of self-discovery.

The Blueprint of Beliefs:

Your beliefs form the architectural design of your identity. They shape your worldview, guide your decisions, and influence your interactions. To know yourself is to unravel the blueprint of your beliefs, understanding the pillars upon which your perspectives stand.

Belief Clarification Exercise

Engage in a belief clarification exercise. Identify core beliefs that influence your thoughts and actions. Question the origin of these beliefs and assess whether they align with your authentic self. This process allows you to distinguish inherited beliefs from those authentically embraced.

The Tapestry of Relationships:

The mirror of self-discovery reflects not only an individual but also the reflections cast by relationships. Your connections with others serve as mirrors that illuminate facets of your own identity.

To know yourself is to navigate the interplay between individuality and interconnectedness.

Relationship Reflections

Consider the reflections mirrored in your relationships. What do your connections reveal about your values, boundaries, and emotional patterns? Reflect on how each relationship, be it familial, romantic, or platonic, contributes to the mosaic of your self-awareness.

The Alchemy of Change:

Self-discovery is not a stagnant state but an ever-evolving journey. To know yourself is to acknowledge the alchemy of change—a continual process of growth, adaptation, and transformation. Embrace the fluidity of your identity as you navigate the currents of life.

Change Affirmation Practice

Incorporate a change affirmation practice into your daily routine. Affirm your openness to growth, resilience in the face of change, and acceptance of the evolving nature of your identity. This practice becomes a mantra that aligns your mindset with the dynamic essence of self-discovery.

The Unveiling Continues:

As you embark on the quest within, the unveiling of self-discovery unfolds as a perpetual journey. How well do you know yourself? This question, rather than having a singular answer, becomes a mantra that echoes through each chapter of your life.

In the subsequent chapters of this odyssey, we will delve deeper into specific facets of self-discovery, exploring the realms of emotions, purpose, and the symbiotic dance between the individual and the cosmos. The quest within is an ever-deepening exploration, and the canvas of self-awareness awaits the strokes of revelation.

CHAPTER 2

Rediscovering Faith and Spirituality

In the vast tapestry of self-discovery, the thread of faith intertwines with the fabric of our existence, weaving a narrative that transcends the boundaries of the known. This chapter serves as a beacon, inviting you to embark on a profound journey to rediscover the roots of faith and spirituality. Recognize these elements not merely as concepts but as transformative forces anchoring your odyssey toward unlocking the divine power within.

Nurturing the Seeds of Faith Within:

Faith, often described as the substance of things hoped for, the evidence of things unseen, stands as a foundational pillar in the exploration of the divine. It extends beyond religious connotations, manifesting as a universal force connecting individuals to something greater than themselves. Reflect deeply on the seeds of faith sown within your consciousness. What experiences, teachings, or moments have left an indelible mark, shaping your understanding of faith?

Reflective Exercise: The Seeds of Faith Journal

Embark on the creation of a "Seeds of Faith Journal," a sacred repository documenting pivotal moments contributing to the growth of your faith. Chronicle instances of strength, resilience, and moments of awe or inspiration. This exercise becomes a living testament to the dynamic and evolving nature of your spiritual journey.

The Historical Tapestry of Faith:

As we delve into the exploration of faith, let's trace the historical threads that have woven the rich tapestry of beliefs and spiritual practices. From ancient civilizations to modern times, faith has been an enduring companion on the human journey. Consider the monumental shifts in religious paradigms, the emergence of profound spiritual leaders, and the evolution of sacred texts. Understanding the historical context enriches our appreciation of the diverse manifestations of faith.

Practical Steps to Strengthen Your Faith:

Faith is no passive bystander; it demands intentional nurturing. Delve into practical strategies aimed at fortifying the foundation of your faith, recognizing it as a dynamic force propelling you forward.

Strategies for Strengthening Faith:
1. Cultivate a Spirit of Gratitude:

Acknowledge both the blessings and challenges in your life with gratitude. Gratitude acts as a transformative force, fostering a positive mindset and strengthening your connection with the divine.

2. Engage in Spiritual Practices:

Whether through prayer, meditation, or contemplation, incorporate spiritual practices into your daily routine. These rituals serve as touchpoints, grounding you on your faith journey.

3. Seek Guidance from Spiritual Texts:

Explore sacred texts or writings resonating with your beliefs. Draw wisdom from these sources to deepen your understanding and connection with your faith, forging a symbiotic relationship with timeless truths.

4. Connect with a Spiritual Community:

Immerse yourself in a community that shares your faith or spiritual values. Collective worship and shared experiences enhance the communal aspect of faith, fostering a sense of unity and support.

The Transformative Role of Faith in Your Journey:

Faith, as a guiding light, illuminates the path to self-realization and divine connection. It is a force that not only instills courage in times of adversity but also provides a profound sense of purpose and meaning to your existence.

Faith in Art and Literature:

Explore how faith has manifested in the realms of art and literature throughout the ages. From the masterpieces of religious art to the profound expressions of faith in literature, these creations serve as a testament to the enduring impact of spiritual beliefs on human creativity. Dive into the works of artists and writers who have channeled the essence of faith into their masterful creations.

Reflecting on Personal Experiences:

Embark on a retrospective journey through the chapters of your life, identifying moments where your faith was tested, strengthened, or transformed. Reflect deeply on how these experiences have shaped your character, contributing richly to your spiritual growth.

The Intersection of Faith and Science:

Engage in an exploration of the intersection between faith and science. While seemingly disparate, these realms often converge in the quest for understanding the mysteries of existence. Investigate how individuals, throughout history, have reconciled their spiritual beliefs with scientific inquiry, showcasing the compatibility and mutual enrichment of faith and scientific exploration.

The Intersection of Faith and Spirituality:

While faith often finds its expression in religious traditions, spirituality transcends the confines of organized practices. Acknowledge the delicate interplay between faith and spirituality, understanding that the latter is a deeply personal and subjective aspect of your connection with the divine.

The Ever-Evolving Nature of Faith:

As you delve into the roots of your faith, embrace its ever-evolving nature. Faith is a dynamic force that adapts, grows, and transforms in response to your life experiences and the unfolding chapters of your spiritual journey. Allow it to be a living, breathing entity that evolves with you.

Faith in Cultural Traditions:

Examine how faith has interwoven with cultural traditions across the globe. From ancient rituals to contemporary celebrations, cultural practices often carry profound spiritual significance. Uncover the beauty of diversity in faith expressions, discovering how different cultures have woven threads of belief into the fabric of their identities.

Embracing Faith as a Cornerstone:

Within this expansive chapter, rediscover faith as an unwavering cornerstone in your relationship with the divine. Embrace it not as a static concept but as a dynamic force that anchors and propels you toward a deeper understanding of the divine power within.

Faith in Contemporary Challenges:

Explore how faith grapples with and navigates contemporary challenges. From the complexities of modern life to ethical dilemmas, faith continues to be a guiding force. Investigate how individuals and communities draw on their spiritual beliefs to address and find meaning in the face of present-day issues.

In the ensuing chapters the odyssey will continue, reaching into the inner journey to divine connection and unlocking the alchemical power of rituals and symbolism. As you immerse yourself in the rediscovery of faith, let its transformative energy be the guiding force leading you toward the luminous core of your spiritual awakening.

CHAPTER 3

Embracing the Symphony of Emotions

In the grand tapestry of self-discovery, emotions emerge as vibrant threads weaving intricate patterns within the canvas of our being. Embracing the symphony of emotions is an essential aspect of understanding ourselves more deeply. This chapter invites you to explore the rich landscape of your feelings, recognizing them as powerful messengers guiding you on the journey of self-awareness.

The Language of Emotions:

Emotions are the language of the soul—a nuanced expression of our inner world. Each emotion carries a unique resonance, conveying messages about our desires, fears, and needs. To embark on the journey of self-discovery is to learn the language of your emotions, deciphering the whispers of your heart.

Emotional Mapping Exercise:

Begin by creating an emotional map. Identify and label different emotions you experience. Consider the circumstances that trigger these emotions and the physical sensations accompanying them. This exercise serves as a compass, guiding you through the landscape of your emotional terrain.

Navigating the Spectrum:

The spectrum of emotions is vast and diverse, ranging from joy and love to sadness and anger. Each emotion serves a purpose, offering valuable insights into the layers of your psyche. To know yourself is to navigate this spectrum with curiosity and acceptance, acknowledging the validity of every emotional hue.

Journaling Your Emotional Landscape:

Maintain an emotional journal to track the ebb and flow of your feelings. Record moments of emotional intensity, noting the triggers and the narrative surrounding each emotion. This practice fosters a deeper connection with your emotional self.

Embracing Vulnerability:

Vulnerability is the gateway to authentic emotional expression. It is the courage to feel deeply, to acknowledge the tender aspects of your heart. To know yourself is to embrace vulnerability, recognizing that it is through the rawness of emotion that genuine connection with yourself and others blossoms.

Vulnerability in Action:

Engage in intentional acts of vulnerability. Share your authentic feelings with someone you trust, expressing your joys, fears, and uncertainties. Through vulnerability, you cultivate emotional intimacy and strengthen your understanding of your own emotional landscape.

Understanding Emotional Triggers:

Emotional triggers are gateways to deeper self-awareness. They are cues that unveil unresolved aspects of your past, unmet needs, or areas requiring healing. To know yourself is to explore the roots of your emotional triggers, peeling back the layers to reveal the narratives embedded within.

Trigger Reflection Exercise:

Identify recurring emotional triggers in your life. Reflect on the origins of these triggers and their connection to past experiences. This introspective exercise illuminates the emotional imprints that shape your present responses.

The Dance of Yin and Yang:

Emotions exist in dynamic equilibrium—an interplay of opposing forces. To know yourself is to embrace the dance of yin and yang within your emotional landscape. It is the harmonious integration of joy and sorrow, love and anger, creating a symphony that resonates with the complexity of the human experience.

Balancing Ritual:

Develop a balancing ritual that acknowledges and embraces both positive and challenging emotions. This could be a mindfulness practice, creative expression, or simply taking a moment to honor the ebb and flow of emotions within you.

Cultivating Emotional Intelligence:

Emotional intelligence is the ability to navigate and understand emotions, both within yourself and in others. To know yourself is to cultivate emotional intelligence, enhancing your capacity to respond to emotions with wisdom and empathy.

Emotional Intelligence Exercises:
1. Mindful Breathing:

Practice mindful breathing to anchor yourself in the present moment when experiencing strong emotions. This simple yet powerful exercise fosters emotional regulation.

2. Empathy Building:

Engage in empathy-building activities, such as reading literature from diverse perspectives or actively listening to others' emotional experiences. This broadens your emotional vocabulary and enhances empathy.

Emotions as Signposts:

Emotions are signposts guiding you toward alignment with your authentic self. They indicate when you are in harmony with your values and when you might be veering off course. To know yourself is to heed these emotional signposts, allowing them to illuminate the path toward authenticity.

Values Alignment Check:

Regularly assess your emotions in relation to your values. Are your emotional responses in alignment with what truly matters to you? This check ensures that your actions and choices resonate with your authentic self.

The Transformative Power of Emotional Expression:

Emotional expression is a catalyst for transformation. To know yourself is to find avenues for expressing your emotions authentically. Whether through art, writing, or verbal communication, expressing your emotions liberates their energy and facilitates self-discovery.

Expressive Arts Exploration:

Experiment with expressive arts as a means of emotional expression. This could involve painting, writing, dancing, or any form of creative expression that resonates with you. Allow the process to unfold organically, uncovering hidden facets of your emotional landscape.

Honoring the Sacred Pause:

In the rush of daily life, the sacred pause is a moment of intentional stillness—an opportunity to tune into your emotions without judgment. To know yourself is to honor the sacred pause, creating space for reflection and emotional integration.

Mindful Pause Practice:

Incorporate mindful pauses throughout your day. Set aside moments to check in with your emotions, observing them without attachment. This practice fosters a deepening awareness of the emotional currents within you.

Embracing Complexity:

Your emotional landscape is intricate, shaped by a myriad of influences. To know yourself is to embrace the complexity of your emotions, acknowledging that they are fluid, multifaceted, and subject to change.

Emotional Complexity Meditation:

Engage in an emotional complexity meditation. Reflect on the layers of your emotions, recognizing their interconnectedness. This meditation deepens your understanding of the subtle nuances within your emotional world.

Conclusion: The Melody of Self-Discovery

As you traverse the symphony of emotions within, remember that each note contributes to the melody of self-discovery. Embrace the highs and lows, the crescendos and decrescendos, for they are integral to the beautiful composition of your authentic self.

CHAPTER 4

Purpose and Passion:

Navigating the Landscape of Your Calling

In the journey of self-discovery, the quest for purpose and passion stands as a pivotal chapter. Understanding your calling and aligning with your passions can be transformative, guiding you toward a more fulfilling and meaningful existence. This chapter delves into the exploration of purpose, the cultivation of passion, and the symbiotic relationship between the two.

Unveiling Your Purpose:

Purpose is the North Star that illuminates your life's path, providing direction and meaning. To know yourself is to unveil your purpose—a journey that involves introspection, exploration, and a deep connection with your values.

Purpose-Clarification Exercises:
1. Values Inventory:

Identify and prioritize your core values. Your purpose often aligns with what matters most to you. This exercise serves as a foundation for understanding the guiding principles that shape your purpose.

2. Impact Reflection:

Reflect on the impact you want to make in the world. Consider the positive changes you aspire to create in your life and the lives of others. This reflection helps unveil the broader purpose that fuels your journey.

The Intersection of Passion and Purpose:

Passion is the driving force that propels you toward your purpose. To know yourself is to explore the intersection of passion and purpose, recognizing that your deepest joys often align with the contributions you are meant to make in the world.

Passion Mapping:

Create a passion map that identifies activities, causes, or fields that ignite a strong sense of joy and fulfillment within you. This visual representation serves as a compass, guiding you toward the areas where your passion and purpose converge.

Aligning Your Daily Choices:

Living in alignment with your purpose requires conscious choices in your daily life. To know yourself is to assess how well your daily activities, relationships, and commitments align with your overarching purpose.

Purposeful Decision-Making:

Before making significant decisions, consider how they align with your purpose. This practice ensures that your choices resonate with your authentic self and contribute to the fulfillment of your broader mission.

Embracing Growth and Learning:

The journey of purpose and passion is an evolving process that involves continuous growth and learning. To know yourself is to embrace the idea that your purpose may evolve, and new passions may emerge as you navigate different seasons of life.

Lifelong Learning Plan:

Develop a lifelong learning plan that aligns with your purpose and passions. Whether it's acquiring new skills, pursuing education, or engaging in personal development, this plan fosters continuous growth aligned with your evolving self.

Overcoming Obstacles:

The pursuit of purpose and passion is not without challenges. To know yourself is to anticipate and overcome obstacles that may arise on your journey, recognizing them as opportunities for growth.

Resilience Building:

Cultivate resilience by viewing obstacles as stepping stones rather than barriers. Develop coping strategies, seek support when needed, and view challenges as integral parts of your journey toward purpose and passion.

Collaborative Purpose:

Your purpose often intertwines with the collective, contributing to a greater societal or communal goal. To know yourself is to recognize the interconnected nature of purpose and the potential for collaborative efforts to create positive change.

Community Engagement:

Engage with communities or causes that align with your purpose. Collaborative efforts amplify the impact of your contributions and foster a sense of shared purpose.

Passion as a Compass:

Passion serves as a reliable compass, guiding you toward the activities and pursuits that bring genuine joy. To know yourself is to listen to the whispers of passion, recognizing the cues that lead you toward a more fulfilling life.

Passion-Driven Projects:

Initiate projects or endeavors driven by passion. These could be personal projects, creative pursuits, or activities that align with your passions. The joy derived from these endeavors becomes a guiding force toward purposeful living.

The Holistic Self:

Understanding your purpose and passion involves embracing the holistic nature of your being. To know yourself is to acknowledge and integrate the physical, emotional, mental, and spiritual dimensions that collectively shape your identity.

Holistic Well-Being Practices:

Incorporate practices that nurture your holistic well-being. This may include physical exercise, mindfulness, emotional expression, and spiritual rituals. Balancing these dimensions enhances your self-awareness and supports your journey toward purpose and passion.

Legacy Building:

To know yourself is to consider the legacy you wish to leave behind. Purpose and passion are intertwined with the impact you make on the world, and understanding the legacy you want to create shapes your actions in the present.

Legacy Reflection:

Reflect on the legacy you aspire to build. Consider the positive contributions you want to be remembered for and the enduring impact you hope to leave on future generations. This reflection serves as a guiding principle for aligning your actions with your desired legacy.

Conclusion: The Harmonious Dance of Purpose and Passion

As you navigate the landscape of your calling, remember that purpose and passion are not static destinations but dynamic, evolving facets of your self-discovery journey. To know yourself is to engage in the harmonious dance of purpose and passion, embracing the transformative power they hold in shaping a life of deep meaning and fulfillment.

CHAPTER 5

The Symbiotic Dance

Individuality and Interconnectedness

In the intricate tapestry of self-discovery, the dance between individuality and interconnectedness forms a profound and nuanced expression of our existence. This chapter explores the delicate balance between embracing one's unique identity and recognizing the interconnected threads that bind us to the larger cosmos.

Embracing Individuality:

Individuality is the fingerprint of the soul—a unique expression of your essence that sets you apart in the vast mosaic of humanity. To know yourself is to embrace and celebrate your individuality, recognizing the distinctive qualities that make you who you are.

Individuality Reflection:

Engage in a reflection on your individuality. Consider the traits, talents, and perspectives that distinguish you from others. Embrace the beauty of your uniqueness, understanding that it contributes to the richness of the collective human experience.

The Quest for Authenticity:

Authenticity is the compass that guides you to your true self. To know yourself is to embark on a quest for authenticity, shedding societal expectations and embracing the unfiltered expression of your thoughts, emotions, and aspirations.

Authenticity Manifesto:

Craft a personal authenticity manifesto—a set of guiding principles that align with your true self. This manifesto serves as a reminder to stay true to your authentic identity in various aspects of life.

Navigating Social Constructs:

While celebrating individuality, the dance with interconnectedness involves navigating societal constructs and cultural influences. To know yourself is to critically examine external expectations, understanding how they shape your perceptions and choices.

Deconstructing Social Conditioning:

Conduct a self-audit of social conditioning. Identify beliefs or behaviors that may be a product of societal expectations rather than authentic self-expression. Deconstructing these influences empowers you to live in alignment with your true values.

Interconnected Threads:

The interconnectedness of all life is a fundamental truth that transcends individuality. To know yourself is to recognize the threads of connection that bind you to others, nature, and the cosmos.

Interconnectedness Meditation:

Practice an interconnectedness meditation. Visualize the threads of connection extending from your heart to the hearts of those around you, expanding further to encompass all living beings. This meditation fosters a sense of unity and compassion.

The Dance of Relationships:

Relationships serve as mirrors reflecting both individuality and interconnectedness. To know yourself is to engage in conscious, meaningful relationships that honor both your unique identity and the shared humanity you embody.

Relationship Audit:

Conduct a relationship audit, evaluating the dynamics of your connections. Consider how each relationship either supports or hinders the expression of your authentic self. Cultivate relationships that nurture your individuality while fostering a sense of belonging.

The Ripple Effect:

Every action, thought, and emotion creates ripples that reverberate through the interconnected web of existence. To know yourself is to recognize the impact of your choices on the collective, understanding the responsibility that comes with interconnected living.

Ripple Effect Journaling:

Maintain a ripple effect journal. Reflect on the consequences—intended or unintended—of your actions on others and the world. This practice deepens your awareness of the interconnected web of cause and effect.

Empathy and Compassion:

Empathy and compassion are bridges that span the gap between individuality and interconnectedness. To know yourself is to cultivate empathy for others' unique journeys while recognizing the shared human experience.

Empathy-Building Exercises:
1. Perspective-Taking:

Engage in perspective-taking exercises. Put yourself in others' shoes to understand their experiences and emotions. This practice enhances empathy and strengthens the bonds of interconnectedness.

2. Random Acts of Kindness:

Perform random acts of kindness as a way to express compassion. Small gestures contribute to a positive ripple effect in the interconnected fabric of human interactions.

Environmental Consciousness:

Interconnectedness extends beyond human relationships to include our connection with the environment. To know yourself is to cultivate environmental consciousness, recognizing the impact of individual choices on the well-being of the planet.

Eco-Conscious Lifestyle:

Adopt an eco-conscious lifestyle. Reduce your ecological footprint by making sustainable choices in consumption, waste reduction, and conservation. This practice reflects an understanding of the interconnected relationship between humanity and the environment.

Spirituality and Unity:

Spirituality often serves as a gateway to the profound sense of unity that transcends individuality. To know yourself is to explore the spiritual dimensions of interconnectedness, recognizing the divine essence that unites all beings.

Spiritual Unity Meditation:

Engage in a spiritual unity meditation. Connect with the universal energy or divine presence that transcends individual identity. This practice deepens your spiritual understanding of interconnectedness.

Cultivating Global Citizenship:

To know yourself is to extend your sense of interconnectedness to a global scale. Cultivating global citizenship involves recognizing the shared challenges and opportunities that bind humanity as a whole.

Global Awareness Initiatives:

Participate in global awareness initiatives. Stay informed about global issues, contribute to positive change, and foster a sense of responsibility toward the well-being of the global community.

Conclusion: The Symphony of Oneness

As you navigate the dance between individuality and interconnectedness, remember that the symphony of oneness is woven from the harmonious interplay of unique melodies. To know yourself is to embrace the dance, celebrating both the solo and the ensemble of existence.

CHAPTER 6

The Journey of Self-Love and Compassion

In the process of self-discovery, the journey of self-love and compassion transforms the base elements of doubt and self-criticism into the gold of profound self-acceptance. This chapter delves into the transformative power of cultivating love and compassion for oneself, an essential journey toward unlocking the divine power within.

Recognizing Your Inherent Worth:

To know yourself is to recognize your inherent worth, independent of external achievements or societal validation. The journey of self-love begins with acknowledging the fundamental truth that you are worthy of love and compassion simply by virtue of being.

Affirmation Ritual:

Incorporate a daily affirmation ritual. Affirm your inherent worthiness by stating phrases such as "I am deserving of love," and "I accept myself unconditionally." This practice sets a positive tone for your day.

Embracing Imperfections:

Self-love flourishes in the soil of self-acceptance, imperfections and all. To know yourself is to embrace your flaws as integral parts of your unique tapestry, recognizing that they contribute to the beauty of your authenticity.

Imperfection Celebration:

Celebrate your imperfections through a creative outlet. Create art, poetry, or a written piece that honors the beauty in your flaws. This celebratory practice reframes imperfections as unique expressions of your individuality.

The Language of Self-Compassion:

Self-compassion is the gentle language spoken to the soul during times of difficulty. To know yourself is to cultivate self-compassion, offering kindness and understanding to yourself in moments of struggle or pain.

Compassionate Self-Talk Journal:

Maintain a compassionate self-talk journal. Record instances where you demonstrate self-compassion in challenging situations. This journal serves as a testament to your evolving capacity for kindness toward yourself.

Setting Healthy Boundaries:

Self-love involves setting and maintaining healthy boundaries that honor your needs and well-being. To know yourself is to recognize your limits and communicate them assertively, fostering a sense of safety and self-respect.

Boundary-Setting Practice:

Practice setting boundaries in various aspects of your life. This could include communicating your needs in relationships, managing work-life balance, and prioritizing self-care. Consistent boundary-setting reinforces a foundation of self-love.

Forgiveness as Liberation:

Forgiveness is a transformative act of self-love, releasing the burden of resentment and creating space for healing. To know yourself is to embark on the journey of forgiveness, both for others and, crucially, for yourself.

Forgiveness Ritual:

Engage in a forgiveness ritual. Write a letter of forgiveness to yourself, acknowledging past mistakes or perceived shortcomings. This ritual allows you to release self-imposed guilt and embrace the healing power of self-forgiveness.

Nurturing Mind, Body, and Spirit:

Self-love extends to the holistic care of mind, body, and spirit. To know yourself is to engage in nurturing practices that support your overall well-being, fostering a harmonious connection between these essential dimensions.

Holistic Self-Nurturing Plan:

Develop a holistic self-nurturing plan. Include practices such as regular exercise, nutritious eating, mindfulness, and spiritual rituals. This plan becomes a commitment to nurturing every aspect of your being.

Cultivating Gratitude for Self:

Gratitude is a potent concoction for self-love, fostering appreciation for the intricacies of your existence. To know yourself is to cultivate gratitude for the unique qualities, experiences, and lessons that shape your journey.

Gratitude Journaling:

Maintain a gratitude journal specifically focused on self-appreciation. Regularly write down aspects of yourself for which you are grateful. This practice instills a positive self-perception and reinforces the foundation of self-love.

Radiating Compassion Outward:

Self-love creates a ripple effect that extends to the way you interact with others and the world. To know yourself is to radiate compassion outward, recognizing the interconnectedness of all beings in the shared tapestry of existence.

Random Acts of Kindness to Self:

Engage in random acts of kindness directed toward yourself. Whether it's taking a leisurely walk, enjoying a favorite meal, or allocating time for a hobby, these acts of self-kindness contribute to the wellspring of self-love.

The Healing Power of Self-Love:

Self-love is a healing balm that soothes wounds, fosters resilience, and nourishes the spirit. To know yourself is to embrace the healing power of self-love, recognizing it as a transformative force on the journey to unlocking the divine power within.

Healing Visualization:

Practice a healing visualization. Imagine a warm, radiant light enveloping you, symbolizing the transformative power of self-love. Visualize this light permeating every aspect of your being, bringing healing and renewal.

Conclusion: The Alchemical Transformation

As you embark on the alchemical journey of self-love and compassion, remember that the process is ongoing—an ever-unfolding exploration of the profound connection between the individual self and the boundless, compassionate universe.

CHAPTER 7

Mindfulness and the Art of Present Living

In the tapestry of self-discovery, the thread of mindfulness weaves a profound connection to the present moment, unraveling the past and casting a gentle light on the future. This chapter explores the transformative practice of mindfulness, a gateway to unlocking the divine power within by anchoring the self in the richness of each passing moment.

Understanding Mindfulness:

To know yourself is to understand the essence of mindfulness—an intentional awareness of the present moment without judgment. The journey of mindfulness involves cultivating a deep connection to the now, unraveling the layers of distraction to reveal the core of authentic being.

Mindfulness Definition:

Reflect on your understanding of mindfulness. Define what mindfulness means to you personally, recognizing its potential to enhance self-awareness and deepen the experience of life.

The Power of Breath:

Breath serves as an anchor to the present moment, a rhythmic reminder of the continuous dance between self and the universe. To know yourself is to harness the power of breath, using it as a gateway to mindfulness and inner peace.

Breath Awareness Meditation:

Engage in a breath awareness meditation. Focus your attention on the inhalation and exhalation, observing each breath without attempting to control it. This practice grounds you in the present and cultivates a sense of calm.

Observing Thoughts and Emotions:

Mindfulness involves observing thoughts and emotions without attachment, allowing them to arise and pass like clouds in the sky. To know yourself is to develop the skill of detached observation, fostering a deeper understanding of the inner landscape.

Mindful Journaling:

Maintain a mindful journal. Record your thoughts and emotions without judgment, observing them as they come and go. This practice enhances self-awareness and promotes a non-reactive relationship with the fluctuations of the mind.

Cultivating Presence in Daily Activities:

Mindfulness extends beyond formal meditation to infuse daily activities with a sense of presence. To know yourself is to cultivate mindfulness in routine tasks, elevating the ordinary to the extraordinary through focused awareness.

Mindful Eating Exercise:

Practice mindful eating. Choose a meal and savor each bite, paying attention to the flavors, textures, and sensations. This exercise transforms a daily activity into a mindfulness practice, fostering a connection to the nourishment of both body and soul.

The Art of Slow Living:

Mindfulness invites a shift from the hurried pace of modern life to the art of slow living—an intentional embrace of the present moment. To know yourself is to explore the transformative power of slowing down, savoring each moment with reverence.

Slow Living Ritual:

Incorporate a slow living ritual into your routine. This could be a daily walk without haste, a leisurely reading session, or dedicated time for quiet contemplation. Slow living becomes a mindful choice to savor the richness of each experience.

Gratitude as a Mindful Practice:

The practice of gratitude aligns harmoniously with mindfulness, directing attention to the blessings of the present moment. To know yourself is to cultivate gratitude as a mindful practice, fostering an appreciation for the abundance that surrounds you.

Gratitude Walk:

Embark on a gratitude walk. As you walk, consciously express gratitude for the elements of nature, the support of loved ones, and the simple joys of existence. This practice enhances mindfulness and deepens the connection to the present.

Mindfulness in Relationships:

Mindfulness extends its transformative touch to relationships, fostering deeper connections through present listening and empathetic presence. To know yourself is to integrate mindfulness into your interactions, creating spaces of genuine connection.

Mindful Listening Exercise:

Practice mindful listening in conversations. Focus your attention on the speaker without formulating responses in advance. This exercise enhances the quality of communication and fosters a deeper understanding of others.

Embracing Silence and Stillness:

In the sanctuary of silence and stillness, mindfulness finds its purest expression. To know yourself is to embrace moments of quiet reflection, allowing the mind to settle and revealing the serenity that resides within.

Mindful Silence Retreat:

Engage in a mindful silence retreat, dedicating a day or a few hours to silent contemplation. This practice provides a profound experience of stillness, inviting insights and a heightened awareness of the present moment.

Mindfulness and Self-Compassion:

Mindfulness intertwines with self-compassion, creating a nurturing space for acceptance and kindness toward oneself. To know yourself is to infuse mindfulness with self-compassion, recognizing the impermanence of thoughts and emotions.

Loving-Kindness Meditation:

Practice loving-kindness meditation. Extend wishes of well-being to yourself and others, fostering a compassionate mindset. This practice complements mindfulness, cultivating a heart-centered awareness of the interconnected web of existence.

Conclusion: The Ever-Present Now

As you delve into the practice of mindfulness, remember that each breath, each thought, and each moment holds the potential for profound self-discovery. To know yourself is to immerse in the ever-present now, where the beauty of existence unfolds in its most authentic form.

CHAPTER 8

The Sacred Art of Introspection

In the profound exploration of self-discovery, introspection stands as the sacred art of diving deep into the ocean of your inner being. This chapter illuminates the transformative power of introspection—a journey that unveils the layers of your soul, reveals hidden truths, and paves the way for a profound connection with the divine within.

Understanding Introspection:

To know yourself is to understand the essence of introspection—a deliberate and contemplative process of self-examination. The journey of introspection involves peeling away the layers of conditioning, societal influences, and external expectations to reveal the authentic self.

Introspection Definition:

Reflect on your understanding of introspection. Define what introspection means to you personally, recognizing its potential to unveil the depths of your thoughts, emotions, and beliefs.

Creating Sacred Space for Introspection:

Introspection thrives in the embrace of sacred space—a quiet refuge where you can delve into the recesses of your mind and spirit. To know yourself is to create a sacred space for introspection, free from distractions and conducive to self-reflection.

Sacred Space Ritual:

Establish a sacred space for introspection. Choose a designated area, adorn it with meaningful symbols, and make it a haven for quiet contemplation. This ritual enhances the introspective journey by fostering a sense of serenity and focus.

The Art of Journaling:

Journaling becomes the brush with which you paint the canvas of your inner world during the introspective journey. To know yourself is to embrace the art of journaling—a practice that captures the nuances of your thoughts, emotions, and revelations.

Introspective Journaling Prompts:
Engage in introspective journaling using prompts such as:

- Reflect on a pivotal life moment and its impact on your journey.

- Explore your core values and how they shape your decisions.

- Contemplate the patterns of behavior that may no longer serve you.

Unraveling the Layers of Beliefs:

Introspection involves unraveling the layers of beliefs that shape your worldview and influence your actions. To know yourself is to question and examine these beliefs, discerning between those that align with your authentic self and those that hinder your growth.

Belief Examination Exercise:

Conduct a belief examination exercise. Identify a belief that influences your thoughts or behaviors. Delve into its origins, assess its relevance, and contemplate whether it aligns with your true self. This exercise fosters clarity and conscious belief alignment.

Exploring the Landscape of Emotions:

The landscape of emotions is vast and varied, and introspection invites you to navigate its terrain with curiosity and compassion. To know yourself is to explore the rich tapestry of your emotions, understanding their origins and embracing their transformative potential.

Emotion Mapping:

Create an emotion map. Chart the various emotions you experience and explore the circumstances triggering each emotion. This visual representation deepens self-awareness and facilitates a more nuanced understanding of emotional responses.

Tracing the Threads of Life Experiences:

Life experiences weave the tapestry of your identity, and introspection involves tracing the threads that connect past, present, and future. To know yourself is to explore the impact of significant life experiences on your beliefs, values, and self-perception.

Life Timeline Reflection:

Create a life timeline reflecting key milestones, challenges, and transformative moments. Analyze the interconnectedness of these experiences and their influence on your present self. This reflective exercise illuminates patterns and growth.

Cultivating Self-Compassion in Introspection:

As you navigate the depths of introspection, self-compassion becomes a guiding light—a gentle embrace that soothes and nurtures. To know yourself is to cultivate self-compassion during the introspective journey, recognizing that self-discovery is a journey of grace.

Loving Presence Meditation:

Incorporate a loving presence meditation into your introspective practice. Imagine a compassionate presence accompanying you as you delve into your inner world. This meditation fosters a sense of warmth and acceptance throughout the introspective process.

Integrating Insights into Daily Life:

The insights gained through introspection find their true value when seamlessly integrated into your daily existence. To know yourself is to apply the wisdom gleaned from introspection, fostering a conscious and purposeful way of living.

Introspective Action Plan:

Develop an introspective action plan. Identify specific insights or realizations from your introspective journey and outline tangible steps to integrate them into your daily life. This action plan serves as a bridge between self-discovery and conscious living.

Balancing Solitude and Connection:

Introspection dances between the solitude that fosters self-discovery and the connection that enriches the human experience. To know yourself is to strike a harmonious balance between introspective solitude and meaningful connections with others.

Introspective Retreats and Shared Reflection:

Engage in introspective retreats that provide dedicated time for solitary contemplation. Additionally, participate in shared reflections with like-minded individuals to exchange insights and perspectives. This balance enriches the introspective journey with diverse viewpoints.

Conclusion: The Ongoing Tapestry of Self-Discovery

As you immerse yourself in the sacred art of introspection, recognize that the tapestry of self-discovery is an ongoing masterpiece—a canvas that evolves with each brushstroke of introspective inquiry. To know yourself is to embrace the beauty of this ever-unfolding journey.

CHAPTER 9

The Symphony of Relationships

In the grand orchestration of self-discovery, relationships play a vital and melodic role, contributing to the harmonious composition of your life. This chapter explores the intricate interplay between self-awareness and relationships, inviting you to recognize the transformative power of connection on the journey to unlocking the divine power within.

Understanding the Dynamics of Relationships:

To know yourself is to understand the dynamics of relationships—a complex dance where individuals co-create shared experiences, learn from one another, and mirror aspects of the self. The journey of self-discovery intertwines with the tapestry of relationships, offering reflections and opportunities for growth.

Relationship Reflection Questions:
Reflect on your current understanding of relationships. Consider questions such as:

- How do your relationships contribute to your sense of self?

- What patterns or themes emerge in your interactions with others?

- In what ways do your relationships serve as mirrors for self-awareness?

The Mirror of Relationships:

Relationships serve as mirrors, reflecting both the light and shadows within. To know yourself is to gaze into the mirror of relationships, recognizing the potential for self-discovery and transformation in the dynamics with others.

Mirror Exercise:

Engage in a mirror exercise. Choose a significant relationship and reflect on the qualities you admire and those that trigger discomfort. Consider how these reflections relate to aspects of your own personality or unresolved emotions. This exercise enhances self-awareness through relationship dynamics.

Navigating Healthy Boundaries:

Healthy boundaries form the cornerstone of fulfilling relationships and contribute to the cultivation of self-respect. To know yourself is to navigate and assert healthy boundaries, fostering a sense of balance and mutual respect in your connections with others.

Boundary-Setting Practice:

Practice boundary-setting in relationships. Clearly communicate your needs, values, and limits, while respecting the autonomy and boundaries of others. This practice creates a harmonious space where self-discovery aligns with authentic connection.

Authentic Communication:

Communication is the melody that resonates through relationships, shaping understanding, and fostering connection. To know yourself is to engage in authentic communication, expressing your thoughts and emotions genuinely while empathetically listening to others.

Reflective Communication Journal:

Maintain a reflective communication journal. Document instances of authentic communication, noting the feelings, insights, and connections that arise. This practice enhances self-awareness in how you express yourself and engage with others.

The Dance of Empathy and Understanding:

Empathy is the dance partner of self-awareness, allowing you to step into the shoes of others and broaden your perspective. To know yourself is to cultivate empathy, fostering a deeper understanding of the emotions and experiences of those around you.

Empathy-Building Exercise:

Practice empathy-building exercises. Engage in conversations where you actively listen to others' perspectives and seek to understand their emotions. This exercise broadens your capacity for empathy and enriches the tapestry of your relationships.

Unraveling Relationship Patterns:

Patterns in relationships offer valuable clues to aspects of your own psyche and emotional landscape. To know yourself is to unravel recurring relationship patterns, recognizing the threads that connect your past experiences to your present interactions.

Relationship Pattern Reflection:

Reflect on recurring patterns in your relationships. Identify similarities or themes in your connections with others. Explore how these patterns may be linked to your own beliefs, expectations, or unresolved experiences. This reflection enhances self-awareness and provides insights for growth.

The Impact of Relationships on Self-Image:

Relationships shape the canvas of your self-image, influencing the way you perceive and value yourself. To know yourself is to recognize the impact of relationships on your self-esteem and cultivate connections that uplift and support your authentic self.

Self-Image Enhancement Exercise:

Conduct a self-image enhancement exercise. Identify relationships that positively contribute to your self-image and well-being. Deliberately nurture and prioritize these connections, creating a supportive network that aligns with your journey of self-discovery.

Embracing Relationship Challenges as Opportunities:

Challenges within relationships are invitations for growth, offering opportunities to delve deeper into self-awareness. To know yourself is to embrace relationship challenges as stepping stones, learning from conflicts and using them as catalysts for personal evolution.

Conflict Resolution Practice:

Engage in conflict resolution practices within relationships. Approach conflicts with curiosity and a willingness to understand both perspectives. This practice transforms challenges into opportunities for enhanced self-awareness and strengthened connections.

The Role of Intimacy in Self-Discovery:

Intimacy, both emotional and physical, serves as a crucible for self-discovery, allowing vulnerabilities to be shared and bonds to deepen. To know yourself is to understand the transformative power of intimacy, navigating it with consciousness and respect.

Intimacy Reflection:

Reflect on your experiences of intimacy in relationships. Consider how moments of vulnerability and closeness contribute to self-discovery. This reflection fosters a deeper appreciation for the multifaceted role of intimacy in your journey.

Conclusion: The Melody of Connection

As you immerse yourself in the symphony of relationships, recognize that each connection is a note contributing to the grand composition of your life. To know yourself is to dance harmoniously within the intricate melodies of relationships, celebrating the transformative power of authentic connection.

CHAPTER 10

The Significance of Rituals and Symbolism

In the enchanting tapestry of self-discovery, rituals and symbolism weave threads of profound meaning, offering a gateway to unlock the divine power within. This chapter explores the alchemical synergy between rituals, symbolism, and the journey toward a deeper connection with the divine.

Unveiling the Magic of Rituals:

To know yourself is to recognize the magic woven into the fabric of rituals — a series of intentional and symbolic acts that transcend the mundane, creating a sacred space for self-discovery and communion with the divine.

Personal Ritual Reflection:

Reflect on any personal rituals you currently practice or have experienced. Consider how these rituals contribute to your sense of self, peace, or connection with the sacred. This reflection lays the foundation for understanding the role of rituals in your life.

The Transformative Power of Symbolism:

Symbols are the language of the soul, conveying profound meanings that resonate with the depths of your being. To know yourself is to explore the transformative power of symbolism, deciphering the messages embedded in symbols encountered on your journey.

Symbol Exploration Exercise:

Embark on a symbol exploration exercise. Identify symbols that hold personal significance or resonance for you. Delve into the meanings attributed to these symbols across cultures and traditions. This exercise enhances symbolic awareness and its impact on self-discovery.

Creating Personal Rituals:

Personal rituals become a canvas for self-expression and a pathway to the sacred. To know yourself is to create and imbue personal rituals with intention, infusing them with meaning that aligns with your values and aspirations.

Personal Ritual Creation Guide:

Utilize a personal ritual creation guide. Define the purpose of your ritual, select symbolic elements, and establish a sequence of actions that resonate with your intention. This guide serves as a template for crafting rituals that enrich your self-discovery journey.

Rituals for Self-Reflection and Contemplation:

Rituals that center around self-reflection and contemplation become portals to the inner realms of the self. To know yourself is to engage in rituals that invite stillness, fostering a space for introspection and connection with the divine within.

Rituals for Inner Exploration:

Incorporate rituals for inner exploration into your routine. This could include a morning reflection ritual, an evening gratitude practice, or moments of mindful breathing throughout the day. These rituals cultivate a deeper understanding of the self.

Symbolism in Everyday Life:

Symbols permeate the fabric of everyday life, offering subtle messages and reminders of the sacred. To know yourself is to attune to the symbolism embedded in your surroundings, recognizing the divine whispers woven into the ordinary.

Symbolic Observation Practice:

Practice symbolic observation in your daily life. Pay attention to symbols encountered in nature, art, or even mundane objects. Reflect on the meanings they evoke and consider how they resonate with your inner world. This practice enhances symbolic consciousness.

Rituals for Emotional Release and Healing:

Rituals can serve as vessels for emotional release and healing, providing a cathartic space to express and process emotions. To know yourself is to engage in rituals that honor and transmute the energies of emotions, fostering emotional well-being.

Rituals for Emotional Alchemy:

Develop rituals for emotional alchemy. This could involve journaling as a means of expression, creating art to externalize emotions, or engaging in movement practices for embodied release. These rituals facilitate emotional awareness and healing.

Sacred Symbolism in Art and Creativity:

Art becomes a sacred language, allowing the soul to express itself beyond words. To know yourself is to explore the sacred symbolism within art and creativity, recognizing the transformative power of creative expression.

Creative Symbolism Project:

Undertake a creative symbolism project. Express your inner world through art, whether it's painting, writing, or any other form of creative expression. Reflect on the symbols and themes that emerge, deepening your connection with your creative self.

Rituals for Connection with Nature:

Nature is a sacred sanctuary, and rituals that align with the natural world deepen the connection with the divine. To know yourself is to engage in rituals that honor the rhythms of nature, fostering a sense of harmony and interconnectedness.

Nature Connection Rituals:

Develop rituals for connection with nature. This could involve mindful walks, meditation in natural settings, or rituals celebrating the changing seasons. These rituals align with the natural flow of life, grounding you in the beauty of the present moment.

Symbolism in Dreams and Intuition:

Dreams and intuition become portals to the subconscious, revealing symbolic messages from the deeper self. To know yourself is to explore the symbolism embedded in dreams and intuitive insights, unlocking hidden facets of your psyche.

Dream Symbolism Journal:

Maintain a dream symbolism journal. Record your dreams and intuitive insights, noting recurring symbols and themes. This journal becomes a tool for deciphering the language of your inner world, enhancing self-awareness through symbolic exploration.

Integrating Rituals and Symbolism into Daily Life:

The true alchemy lies in seamlessly integrating rituals and symbolism into the tapestry of daily life, transforming the ordinary into the extraordinary. To know yourself is to weave the magic of these practices into the fabric of your existence.

Daily Integration Plan:

Develop a daily integration plan for rituals and symbolism. Identify specific moments in your routine where you can infuse intentional acts and symbolic awareness. This plan creates a harmonious flow, enriching your daily experience with sacred meaning.

Conclusion: The Alchemical Symphony of Self-Discovery

As you embark on the alchemical journey of rituals and symbolism, recognize the symphony they create—the harmonious blend of intentional acts and meaningful symbols that elevate your self-discovery to a divine crescendo. To know yourself is to dance with the alchemy of rituals and symbolism, unlocking the sacred power within.

CHAPTER 11

The Inner Sanctum of Mindfulness

In the sanctuary of self-discovery, mindfulness becomes the key to unlocking the door to the inner sanctum. This chapter explores the profound practice of mindfulness—a journey into the present moment, where the divine essence of your being unfolds.

Understanding Mindfulness:

To know yourself is to embark on a journey of mindfulness—a practice that transcends the boundaries of time, inviting you to fully engage with the richness of each moment. This section lays the groundwork for understanding the transformative power of mindfulness.

Mindfulness Definition:

Reflect on your current understanding of mindfulness. Define what mindfulness means to you personally, acknowledging its potential to enhance self-awareness, focus, and a deeper connection with the divine.

The Essence of Present-Moment Awareness:

Mindfulness thrives in the essence of present-moment awareness, where the past and future fade, leaving only the vibrant tapestry of the now. To know yourself is to cultivate the art of being fully present, embracing the nuances of each moment.

Present-Moment Awareness Exercise:

Engage in a present-moment awareness exercise. Choose a specific activity, whether it's eating, walking, or breathing, and immerse yourself fully in the experience. This exercise heightens your sensitivity to the present, fostering mindfulness.

Mindful Breathing as a Gateway:

The breath becomes a sacred gateway to mindfulness, anchoring you in the present and connecting you with the rhythm of life. To know yourself is to explore the transformative power of mindful breathing, a practice that grounds and centers the soul.

Mindful Breathing Practice:

Incorporate a mindful breathing practice into your routine. Dedicate moments to focus on your breath, observing its natural flow without judgment. This practice serves as a foundation for mindfulness, creating a sense of calm and presence.

Cultivating Mindful Observation:

Mindful observation is a lens through which the beauty of the present is revealed. To know yourself is to cultivate the art of mindful observation, appreciating the details and subtleties that unfold in every facet of your experience.

Mindful Observation Exercise:

Practice mindful observation in your surroundings. Choose an object, a scene, or even your own thoughts, and observe without attachment or interpretation. This exercise enhances your ability to engage with the present moment in its entirety.

The Dance of Thoughts and Mindfulness:

Mindfulness invites you to dance with your thoughts, observing them as they ebb and flow without becoming entangled. To know yourself is to navigate the dance of thoughts with mindfulness, fostering a detached awareness of the mental landscape.

Mindful Thoughts Reflection:

Reflect on the interplay between mindfulness and your thoughts. Consider how mindfulness allows you to observe thoughts without attachment. This reflection deepens your understanding of the relationship between your inner world and present-moment awareness.

Mindfulness in Daily Activities:

Every activity becomes a canvas for mindfulness, an opportunity to infuse the mundane with sacred presence. To know yourself is to integrate mindfulness into daily activities, transforming routine actions into moments of conscious engagement.

Mindful Daily Activity Plan:

Develop a mindful daily activity plan. Identify routine tasks where you can bring mindfulness, such as washing dishes, walking, or eating. This plan infuses your day with intentional presence, fostering a deeper connection with the ordinary.

Mindfulness and Emotional Regulation:

Mindfulness becomes a refuge during the storms of emotion, providing a space to witness and regulate the ebb and flow of feelings. To know yourself is to embrace mindfulness as a tool for emotional regulation, cultivating a balanced response to inner states.

Mindfulness in Emotional Moments:

Apply mindfulness in moments of heightened emotion. Pause, observe the sensations and thoughts arising, and breathe mindfully. This practice enhances emotional awareness and resilience, allowing you to navigate emotions with conscious presence.

Mindfulness Meditation for Self-Exploration:

Mindfulness meditation becomes a sacred journey into the landscape of your inner being. To know yourself is to engage in mindfulness meditation, a practice that unveils the layers of consciousness and connects you with the divine essence within.

Mindfulness Meditation Guide:

Utilize a mindfulness meditation guide. Design a meditation that aligns with your goals for self-exploration — whether it's cultivating compassion, enhancing self-love, or simply being present. This guide serves as a compass for your inner journey.

Mindfulness and Compassionate Presence:

Compassion is the heart of mindfulness, inviting you to witness your experiences with kindness and non-judgment. To know yourself is to embrace the compassionate presence of mindfulness, fostering a loving connection with the self.

Loving-Kindness Mindfulness Exercise:

Practice a loving-kindness mindfulness exercise. Extend thoughts of well-being and compassion to yourself and others. This exercise nurtures a kind and gentle relationship with the self, deepening the transformative power of mindfulness.

Integrating Mindfulness into Relationships:

Mindfulness extends its embrace to relationships, fostering conscious connections with others. To know yourself is to integrate mindfulness into relationships, creating spaces of presence and understanding in the shared journey of connection.

Mindful Communication in Relationships:

Apply mindful communication in relationships. Engage in conversations with full attention, listening deeply to the words and emotions expressed. This practice enriches the quality of connections, fostering a sense of shared presence.

The Alchemy of Mindful Presence:

Mindful presence becomes an alchemical elixir, transmuting the ordinary into the extraordinary. Embrace each moment with a heightened sense of awareness, allowing the alchemy of mindfulness to reveal the hidden gems within the tapestry of your existence.

Mindfulness as a Daily Ritual:

Transform mindfulness into a daily ritual, weaving it into the fabric of your morning routine, daily tasks, and evening reflections. By making mindfulness a constant companion, you create a sacred rhythm that harmonizes with the melody of your soul.

Deepening the Connection with the Divine Essence:

Mindfulness serves as a bridge to the divine essence within, inviting you to deepen the connection with the sacred core of your being. In moments of stillness and presence, feel the subtle whispers of the divine, guiding you on the path of self-discovery.

Mindful Connection Visualization:

Engage in a mindful connection visualization. Picture a radiant light within your being, symbolizing the divine essence. With each breath, imagine this light expanding, filling every corner of your being. This visualization enhances the sense of oneness with the divine.

Mindfulness and the Sacred Art of Gratitude:

Gratitude becomes a sacred art within the practice of mindfulness, amplifying the beauty of the present moment. Cultivate a grateful heart as you navigate the realms of mindfulness, acknowledging the blessings that unfold in each breath.

Gratitude Mindfulness Journal:

Maintain a gratitude mindfulness journal. Record moments of gratitude during mindful activities or observations. This practice deepens the connection between mindfulness and gratitude, infusing your journey with a sense of appreciation.

Mindfulness Retreats: Immersing in Stillness:

Consider embarking on mindfulness retreats as a way to immerse yourself in prolonged stillness. These retreats offer a sanctuary for deep self-reflection, allowing you to peel away layers and unveil the essence of your true self in the sacred container of mindfulness.

Mindfulness Retreat Planning:

Plan a mindfulness retreat, whether it's a solitary weekend or a guided group experience. Designate specific practices, such as silent walks, meditation sessions, and mindful meals. A mindfulness retreat becomes a pilgrimage into the heart of self-awareness.

Mindfulness and the Symphony of Self-Discovery:

In the symphony of self-discovery, mindfulness contributes a melodic note, harmonizing with the other elements of your journey. Recognize the interconnectedness of mindfulness with introspection, relationships, and spiritual connection, weaving a seamless narrative of self-awareness.

Mindfulness Integration Exercise:

Integrate mindfulness into various aspects of your life consciously. Whether it's infusing mindfulness into your work, creative pursuits, or moments of leisure, this exercise enhances the holistic integration of mindfulness into the fabric of your being.

Conclusion: The Sacred Stillness of Mindfulness

As you immerse yourself in the sacred stillness of mindfulness, recognize it as a gateway to the inner sanctum—a space where the divine essence of your being unfolds. To know yourself is to dance with mindfulness, allowing each moment to be a step in the cosmic rhythm of self-discovery.

CHAPTER 12

The Path of Reflection

In the labyrinth of self-discovery, the path of reflection emerges as a guiding light, illuminating the inner landscapes and unveiling the wisdom hidden within your experiences. This chapter delves into the transformative practice of reflection—a journey inward to gain insights, foster growth, and deepen the connection with the divine.

The Art of Reflective Contemplation:

To know yourself is to engage in the art of reflective contemplation—a deliberate pause to ponder, explore, and discern the meaning woven into the tapestry of your life. Reflective contemplation becomes a sacred mirror, revealing the nuances of your journey.

Reflective Pause Exercise:

Initiate a reflective pause exercise. Set aside dedicated moments to pause and contemplate aspects of your life. This exercise lays the foundation for reflective contemplation, allowing you to connect with the depth of your experiences.

Unveiling Insights through Journaling:

Journaling becomes a sacred vessel for capturing the whispers of your soul. To know yourself is to embark on a journey of journaling, unveiling insights, and weaving a narrative that chronicles the evolution of your thoughts, emotions, and spiritual connection.

Reflective Journaling Guide:

Utilize a reflective journaling guide. Structure your journaling practice to explore specific themes, emotions, or spiritual experiences. This guide serves as a companion, facilitating a more intentional and profound reflection on your inner world.

Navigating the Tapestry of Life Events:

Life events are threads in the grand tapestry of self-discovery. To know yourself is to navigate these threads with mindfulness, recognizing the interconnectedness of events and their role in shaping your character and spiritual journey.

Life Event Reflection Exercise:

Engage in a life event reflection exercise. Select a significant life event and reflect on its impact on your beliefs, values, and spiritual connection. This exercise deepens your understanding of the spiritual lessons embedded in life's tapestry.

Embracing Vulnerability in Reflection:

Vulnerability becomes a gateway to authenticity in the practice of reflection. To know yourself is to embrace vulnerability, allowing yourself to be seen and heard by your own introspection. This authenticity deepens the connection with your true self.

Vulnerability Reflection Practice:

Incorporate vulnerability reflection into your practice. Explore areas of your life where vulnerability has played a role and reflect on the lessons learned. This practice fosters self-acceptance and a compassionate relationship with your vulnerabilities.

The Interplay of Reflection and Gratitude:

Reflection and gratitude intertwine, creating a harmonious dance in the rhythm of self-discovery. To know yourself is to appreciate the interplay between reflection and gratitude, acknowledging the blessings and lessons embedded in your experiences.

Gratitude Reflection Ritual:

Integrate a gratitude reflection ritual into your routine. Before or after moments of reflection, express gratitude for the insights gained and the growth experienced. This ritual enhances the transformative power of both reflection and gratitude.

Reflecting on Relationships:

Relationships serve as mirrors reflecting the facets of your being. To know yourself is to engage in reflective exploration of relationships, discerning the patterns, dynamics, and spiritual connections that contribute to your journey.

Relationship Reflection Questions:

Pose reflective questions about your relationships. Explore how connections with others shape your understanding of yourself and your spirituality. These questions guide you in unraveling the threads of connection woven into the fabric of your life.

The Spiritual Significance of Challenges:

Challenges become sacred opportunities for growth and self-discovery. To know yourself is to recognize the spiritual significance of challenges, viewing them as catalysts for transformation rather than obstacles.

Challenge Reflection and Transformation:

Reflect on past challenges and their transformative impact on your spirituality. Explore how challenges have shaped your resilience, perspective, and connection with the divine. This reflection unveils the spiritual alchemy inherent in facing adversity.

Reflection as a Tool for Intentional Living:

Reflection becomes a compass for intentional living, guiding your choices, actions, and spiritual alignment. To know yourself is to use reflection as a tool for intentional living, ensuring that each step on your journey is aligned with your authentic self.

Intentional Living Reflection Plan:

Create an intentional living reflection plan. Regularly assess your choices and actions through reflective contemplation. This plan cultivates mindfulness in decision-making and enhances the alignment between your spiritual values and daily life.

Conclusion: The Wisdom Unveiled in Reflection

As you tread the path of reflection, recognize it as a sacred pilgrimage into the depths of your being—a journey where the wisdom of your experiences is unveiled. To know yourself is to embrace the transformative power of reflection, allowing it to be a lantern that lights your way on the spiritual quest.

"Now that you have come to know yourself, take a profound gaze into the mirror. What do you see reflected in its glassy surface? As I peer into the mirror, I perceive not just my physical form but an embodiment of infinite awareness—a unique expression of the Almighty within me. It is a reflection that transcends the superficial and delves into the profound essence of my being."

CHAPTER 13

Reflection and the Mirror of Self-Discovery

In the labyrinth of self-discovery, the path of reflection becomes a guiding light, illuminating the inner landscapes and unveiling the wisdom hidden within your experiences. As you tread this path, take a profound gaze into the mirror of reflective contemplation. What do you see reflected in its glassy surface?

Now that you have come to know yourself, the mirror becomes more than a mere reflective device. It transforms into a sacred vessel, capturing the essence of your journey. As you peer into its depths, observe not just your physical form but an embodiment of infinite awareness—a unique expression of the Almighty within you. This reflection transcends the superficial, delving into the profound essence of your being.

Reflective contemplation is the art of engaging with the mirror of self-discovery, allowing the wisdom of your experiences to unfold. Journaling becomes a companion, chronicling the evolving narrative of your thoughts, emotions, and spiritual connection. Navigate the tapestry of life events with mindfulness, recognizing the interconnected threads that shape your character.

Embrace vulnerability in reflection, allowing yourself to be seen and heard by your own introspection. Acknowledge the interplay between reflection and gratitude, appreciating the blessings and lessons embedded in your experiences. Reflect on relationships as mirrors that reveal the facets of your being, and recognize the spiritual significance of challenges as opportunities for growth.

As you reflect on the labyrinth of your journey, the mirror becomes a compass for intentional living. Use reflection as a tool to guide your choices, actions, and spiritual alignment. The mirror of self-discovery is not just a reflection of your physical form; it is a testament to the infinite awareness and unique expression of the Almighty within you.

Now, take a good look in the mirror. What do you see reflected in its glassy surface? When I gaze into the mirror, I perceive the intricate tapestry of my experiences, the vulnerabilities that make me authentic, and the wisdom gained through challenges. It is a reflection that goes beyond the surface, echoing the infinite awareness and divine essence within.

Extend your contemplation to the mirror of gratitude. Express appreciation for the journey—the moments of growth, the lessons learned, and the connections made.

Each reflection in the mirror becomes a brushstroke in the masterpiece of your life.

In the stillness of reflection, let the mirror unveil not just the chapters of your past but also the unwritten pages of your future. As you conclude this journey of self-discovery, let the mirror be a reminder—an ever-present reflection of the profound connection between your earthly existence and the divine power within you. Embrace the beauty of your reflection, for it mirrors not just who you are but the continuous evolution of your soul—a journey that intertwines with the infinite and echoes through eternity.

Scripture Integration:

"I therefore, a prisoner for the Lord, urge you to walk in a manner worthy of the calling to which you have been called, with all humility and gentleness, with patience, bearing with one another in love, eager to maintain the unity of the Spirit in the bond of peace. There is one body and one Spirit—just as you were called to the one hope that belongs to your call—one Lord, one faith, one baptism, one God and Father of all, who is over all and through all and in all." (Ephesians 4:1-6, ESV)

"Anyone who listens to the word but does not do what it says is like someone who looks at his face in a mirror and, after looking at himself, goes away and immediately forgets what he looks like. But whoever looks intently into the perfect law that gives freedom, and continues in it—not forgetting what they have heard but doing it—they will be blessed in what they do." (James 1:23-25, NIV)

Reflecting on the Tapestry of Experience

Your journey is a tapestry woven with threads of joy, sorrow, triumph, and defeat. In the reflection of the mirror, you encounter the intricate patterns that have shaped your character. Each thread represents a unique experience—a moment in time that has contributed to the masterpiece of your life.

Consider the threads of joy that sparkle in the reflection. These are the moments of celebration, accomplishment, and profound happiness. Whether small victories or significant milestones, they add vibrant hues to your tapestry, creating a mosaic of cherished memories.

The threads of sorrow are equally essential. In the mirror, they may appear as shadows, but they hold the depth of your resilience and strength. These are the moments of loss, heartache, and challenges that, despite their difficulty, have become foundational in shaping your character.

As you gaze into the mirror, recognize the threads of triumph—the instances where you overcame obstacles, transcended limitations, and emerged stronger. These threads are the testament to your resilience, determination, and the indomitable spirit within you.

The threads of defeat, too, play a vital role. They are not marks of weakness but reflections of vulnerability and the courage to confront shortcomings. In acknowledging moments of defeat, you embrace humility, paving the way for growth and continuous self-improvement.

The mirror reflects the interwoven threads of relationships—the connections that have profoundly influenced your journey. Whether family, friends, or mentors, these threads create a network of support, love, and shared experiences.

The Spiritual Tapestry

Beyond the tangible threads, the mirror also unveils the spiritual tapestry of your journey. It reflects the moments of divine connection, the whispers of guidance, and the times when faith carried you through challenges. Each spiritual thread adds a dimension of transcendence to your earthly experiences.

In your reflective journal, document the threads of your spiritual journey. Capture moments of profound connection with the divine, instances of spiritual insight, and the lessons learned through prayer and meditation. The spiritual tapestry is a sacred narrative—a testimony to the continuous dialogue between your soul and the divine.

Embracing Vulnerability in Reflection

Vulnerability is a key element in the art of reflection. As you confront your reflection in the mirror, embrace vulnerability as a pathway to authenticity. Allow yourself to be seen in the rawness of your emotions, thoughts, and aspirations.

Reflect on the vulnerabilities that have shaped your journey. These may include moments of doubt, fear, or uncertainty. Instead of viewing vulnerability as a weakness, recognize it as a source of strength. It is through vulnerability that you connect with your authentic self and invite others to do the same.

In your journal, explore the transformative power of vulnerability. Share your reflections on moments when vulnerability became a catalyst for growth and understanding. Consider how embracing vulnerability has deepened your connections with others and fostered a sense of empathy and compassion.

Reflection and Gratitude: A Symbiotic Relationship

Gratitude is intertwined with reflection, creating a symbiotic relationship that enhances the depth of your experiences. In the mirror, gratitude becomes a radiant glow, illuminating the tapestry of your journey with a positive light.

Consider the moments of your life for which you are grateful. These may range from the simple pleasures of everyday life to profound experiences that have left an indelible mark on your soul. In your journal, create a gratitude list—a collection of blessings, lessons, and sources of joy that enrich your tapestry.

Reflect on how gratitude has been a guiding force in your journey. Explore the ways in which expressing gratitude, both in times of abundance and scarcity, has shaped your perspective and contributed to your spiritual well-being. The mirror reflects not only your physical form but also the radiance of a grateful heart.

Relationships as Mirrors: A Reflective Exploration

The people in your life serve as mirrors, reflecting facets of your being that may remain unseen in solitude. Each relationship, whether harmonious or challenging, unveils dimensions of your character and offers opportunities for growth.

Reflect on the relationships that have left a lasting impact on your journey. These may include family members, friends, colleagues, or mentors. Consider the qualities reflected in these mirrors—love, patience, resilience, or areas for self-improvement.

In your journal, engage in a reflective exploration of relationships. Identify the mirrors that have played pivotal roles in your personal and spiritual development. Share insights into the ways in which relationships have contributed to your understanding of self and others.

Acknowledge the challenges encountered in relationships as opportunities for self-refinement. Explore how moments of conflict or misunderstanding have become mirrors, revealing aspects of your communication style, emotional responses, and areas for personal growth.

Challenges as Mirrors: A Spiritual Perspective

Challenges are mirrors that reflect the depth of your resilience, the strength of your faith, and the capacity for transformation. In the mirror of challenges, you encounter opportunities for spiritual growth and self-discovery.

Reflect on the challenges that have shaped your journey. These may encompass a range of experiences, from personal hardships to professional obstacles. Consider the mirrors that challenges present—reflections of your inner strength, perseverance, and ability to navigate adversity.

In your journal, share reflections on specific challenges and the lessons they have imparted. Explore the ways in which challenges have become transformative mirrors, guiding you toward greater self-awareness and a deeper connection with the divine.

Acknowledge the spiritual significance of challenges as catalysts for growth. Consider how moments of struggle have become mirrors of divine intervention, leading you to inner reservoirs of strength and resilience. The mirror reflects not only the hardships endured but also the spiritual triumphs that arise from navigating the storm.

Reflection and Intentional Living

The mirror of self-discovery becomes a compass for intentional living. As you reflect on the tapestry of your experiences, use the mirror to guide your choices, actions, and spiritual alignment. Intentional living is a conscious and purposeful approach to navigating life's journey.

Consider the choices reflected in the mirror of your life. These may include decisions related to career, relationships, personal development, and spiritual practices. Reflect on how each choice aligns with your values, aspirations, and the overarching purpose of your journey.

In your journal, set intentions for intentional living. Define the values and principles that guide your decision-making process. Explore how reflection serves as a tool for aligning your actions with your authentic self and spiritual path.

Acknowledge the power of intention in shaping your reality. The mirror reflects not only the choices made but also the ripple effects of intentional living—a life that resonates with purpose, authenticity, and spiritual fulfillment.

The Mirror of Self-Discovery: A Compass for Spiritual Alignment

As you conclude this extended chapter on reflection, recognize the mirror of self-discovery as a compass for spiritual alignment. The mirror reflects not only the physical form but also the continuous evolution of your soul—a journey that intertwines with the infinite and echoes through eternity.

In the mirror, witness the beauty of your reflection—a unique expression of the Almighty within you. Embrace the wisdom embedded in the tapestry of your experiences, and let the mirror be a reminder of the profound connection between your earthly existence and the divine power within.

Now, take a moment to gaze into the mirror. What do you see reflected in its glassy surface? As you peer into the depths of your own reflection, may you find not only the visage of your physical form but the luminous core of your spiritual awakening—a journey that unfolds in tandem with the divine.

CHAPTER 14

Unleashing Your Divine Power Practical Steps to Manifest Your Objectives

In the grand tapestry of self-discovery, you've uncovered the divine power within, an omnipotent force that shapes your reality. As we culminate this transformative journey, it's time to distill the profound insights into actionable steps, drawing inspiration from Neville Goddard's teachings and the wisdom accumulated throughout our exploration.

In the realm of self-discovery, clarity becomes the guiding light, illuminating the path toward manifesting your deepest desires. Neville Goddard encourages us to identify our truest aspirations and objectives, recognizing that the power within responds most potently to distinct intentions.

1. Reflect on Your Deepest Desires:

Begin your journey by delving into the reservoir of your innermost self. What stirs your heart, ignites your passion, and resonates with the very essence of who you are? Reflect on moments when you felt most alive and connected to your authentic self. These reflections unveil the seeds of your deepest desires.

Reflective Exercise: Desires Discovery Journal

Create a "Desires Discovery Journal" to chronicle the aspirations that surface during your reflections. What themes emerge? What recurring dreams or visions captivate your imagination? This journal serves as a compass, guiding you toward a more profound understanding of your objectives.

2. Define Clear Goals:

Once the tapestry of your desires begins to unfold, crystallize them into clear and concise goals. Clarity is not merely a conceptual exercise; it is a practical and transformative tool that aligns your conscious and subconscious mind with the divine power within.

Goal Clarity Worksheet:

Develop a "Goal Clarity Worksheet" to articulate your objectives in specific terms. Define the desired outcome, set measurable milestones, and establish a timeframe for achievement. This worksheet becomes a roadmap, allowing you to navigate the vast landscape of your aspirations with precision.

The essence of this section lies in the synergy between self-reflection and the intentional definition of your objectives. As you clarify your desires and set clear goals, you are not only envisioning a future but actively engaging with the divine power within, propelling yourself toward the manifestation of your aspirations.

Section 2: Imagination and Visualization
Cultivate Imagination:

Imagination is the palette where the colors of your dreams take shape. Neville Goddard teaches that imagination is not limited by current circumstances; it is the bridge between your present reality and the realm of infinite possibilities. Cultivate your imagination by engaging in creative pursuits, exploring different perspectives, and allowing your mind to wander beyond the constraints of conventional thinking.

Creative Exploration Exercise:

Dedicate time to creative exploration. Whether through art, writing, or any form of self-expression, tap into the boundless realm of imagination. This exercise fosters a flexible and expansive mindset, essential for the vivid visualization that follows.

Visualization Techniques:

Visualization is the conscious act of seeing and feeling the realization of your objectives. It is a powerful tool that aligns your thoughts and emotions with the desired outcome, sending a clear signal to the subconscious mind.

Practice visualization as a daily ritual, immersing yourself in the sensory details of your achieved goals.

Guided Visualization Session:

Create a guided visualization session tailored to your objectives. Close your eyes, breathe deeply, and vividly picture every detail of your success. Engage all your senses, feel the emotions associated with achievement, and let this practice become a magnetic force drawing your desires into your reality.

Section 2 encourages you to embrace the boundless realm of imagination and leverage the transformative power of visualization. As you cultivate these practices, you open the door to a reality shaped by the creative forces within you.

Section 3: Affirmations and Declarations
Powerful Affirmations:

Affirmations are declarations of truth that resonate with the core of your being. Neville Goddard emphasizes the importance of assuming the feeling of your wish being fulfilled. Craft affirmations that encapsulate the essence of your objectives, phrasing them in the present tense as if they are already a reality. Repeat these affirmations consistently to instill them in your consciousness.

Affirmation Crafting Exercise:

Sit in a quiet space and reflect on the core beliefs that align with your objectives. From these beliefs, craft powerful affirmations. Ensure they evoke strong positive emotions and resonate with your inner truth. This exercise solidifies your commitment to the manifestation process.

Speak Your Desires Aloud:

The spoken word carries a unique vibration that reverberates through your being and the universe. Speak your affirmations and desires aloud with conviction. Let the resonance of your voice amplify the energy behind your words, aligning your conscious and subconscious mind with the divine power within.

Daily Affirmation Ritual:

Establish a daily ritual of speaking your affirmations aloud. Choose a specific time, perhaps morning or evening, to reinforce these positive declarations. Consistency is key, as the repetition deepens their impact on your psyche.

Section 3 empowers you to wield the transformative energy of words. Through powerful affirmations and spoken declarations, you shift the narrative of your reality, affirming your objectives with unwavering certainty.

Section 4: Embracing Gratitude
Gratitude for Future Achievements:

Gratitude is a magnetic force that aligns your energy with the abundance of the universe. Neville Goddard teaches that feeling thankful for the realization of your objectives as if they have already occurred sets the stage for their manifestation. Cultivate gratitude for the future achievements you anticipate.

Future Gratitude Journal:

Create a "Future Gratitude Journal" to express gratitude for the achievements you are yet to experience. Write detailed entries, expressing thanks for the unfolding success. This practice amplifies the vibrational frequency of gratitude, attracting your objectives with greater intensity.

Gratitude Journaling:

Journaling is a potent tool for introspection and manifestation. Maintain a gratitude journal where you record blessings, achievements, and positive experiences. Regularly revisit this journal to reinforce a mindset of appreciation and abundance.

Daily Gratitude Ritual:

Integrate a daily gratitude ritual into your routine. Take a few moments each day to reflect on and write down aspects of your life you are grateful for. This simple practice becomes a beacon, guiding your focus toward positivity and attracting the realization of your objectives.

Section 4 invites you to harness the transformative power of gratitude. By expressing thanks for both current blessings and future achievements, you align yourself with the divine flow of abundance.

Section 5: Action and Alignment
Inspired Action:

Action is the bridge between imagination and manifestation. Identify actionable steps that align with your objectives and take intentional, inspired action. This is not merely about busyness but about purposeful movement toward your goals.

Action Alignment Worksheet:

Create an "Action Alignment Worksheet" to map out the steps required to achieve your objectives. Break down large goals into manageable objectives, tasks and set deadlines. This worksheet becomes a dynamic guide, ensuring your actions align with the unfolding vision.

Alignment with Divine Timing:

Trust the divine timing of your manifestations. Recognize that the universe has its own rhythm, and there is an optimal time for the realization of your objectives. Practice patience, remain attuned to the signs and synchronicities around you, and allow the divine plan to unfold.

Divine Timing Reflection:

Reflect on moments in your life when things fell into place seemingly by chance or at the perfect time. Use these reflections as a reminder that there is a divine orchestration at play. Trust the unfolding journey.

Section 5 underscores the importance of intentional action aligned with the divine flow. By taking purposeful steps and trusting divine timing, you co-create with the universe, ensuring that your journey unfolds in harmony with the cosmic design.

Section 6: Cultivating Faith
Unwavering Faith:

Faith is the bedrock upon which manifestations are built. Cultivate unwavering faith in the realization of your objectives. As Neville Goddard states, "Faith is the substance of things hoped for." Hold the unshakeable belief that your objectives are not mere possibilities but inevitable certainties.

Faith Strengthening Affirmations:

Develop affirmations specifically focused on strengthening your faith. Phrases such as "I trust in the divine timing of my manifestations" or "Every step I take is guided by unwavering faith" can fortify your belief in the process.

Overcoming Doubt:

Doubt is a natural companion on the journey of manifestation. Acknowledge moments of doubt without judgment and work on transforming them into renewed faith. Replace doubt with positive affirmations and reminders of past successes.

Doubt-Transformation Exercise:

When doubt arises, engage in a doubt-transformation exercise. Write down the doubts you are experiencing and counter each one with a positive affirmation or a list of past achievements. This practice reshapes your mental landscape, paving the way for unwavering faith.

Section 6 centers on the cultivation of faith—a force that propels your objectives from the realm of possibility to the realm of certainty. By fortifying your belief and overcoming doubt, you become a conduit for the divine power within to work miracles.

Section 7: Integration of Spiritual Practices
Daily Spiritual Practices:

The spiritual practices explored throughout this ebook serve as anchors for your connection with the divine.

Integrate these practices into your daily routine, establishing a sacred space for communion with the higher self.

Holistic Spiritual Routine:

Develop a holistic spiritual routine that incorporates various practices, including meditation, prayer, and self-reflection. Consistency in these practices deepens your connection with the divine power within and aligns your energy with the manifestation of your objectives.

The 4 Elements of You:

Revisit the physical, emotional, mental, and spiritual aspects of yourself. Ensure holistic alignment for a balanced manifestation journey. Acknowledge and nurture each element, recognizing their interconnectedness.

Elemental Alignment Check:

Regularly assess the alignment of the four elements within yourself. Are you tending to your physical well-being, nurturing emotional intelligence, engaging in mental stimulation, and fostering spiritual connection? This introspective practice ensures a harmonious and integrated approach to manifestation.

Section 7 emphasizes the integration of spiritual practices as a foundational aspect of the manifestation journey.

By establishing a consistent spiritual routine and aligning the four elements of your being, you create a fertile ground for the divine power within to flourish.

Conclusion: Your Journey Unfolding

In the culmination of this transformative journey, each section has provided a unique facet of understanding and practical tools for unleashing your divine power. As you reflect on your deepest desires, engage your imagination, affirm your objectives, express gratitude, take inspired action, cultivate faith, and integrate spiritual practices, remember that you are an active participant in the manifestation process.

With the integration of Neville Goddard's teachings and the insights gathered on this odyssey of self-discovery, you stand at the threshold of conscious creation. The divine power within you is not a distant force but a dynamic energy eager to shape your reality. As you embark on this journey, envision your objectives not as distant dreams but as certainties waiting to manifest.

May your path be illuminated by the light of self-awareness, guided by the wisdom of spiritual practices, and empowered by the unwavering faith in your divine essence. In the words of Neville Goddard, "Dare to believe in the reality of your assumption, and watch the world play its part relative to its fulfillment." Your journey of self-discovery has equipped you with the understanding of your divine essence. Now, with practical tools in hand, step boldly into the arena of manifestation. Your objectives are not just possibilities—they are certainties awaiting the perfect alignment of your conscious creation.

Testimony: How Imagination Shapes Your Destiny

In the midst of my life's journey, I encountered a significant financial challenge. The lease option to purchase the property I was in was approaching its end, and time was running out rapidly. The original building owners granted me an extension, but I was in dire need of selling the property swiftly to secure any financial benefits. With the clock ticking, I found solace by sitting on my bed, in quiet contemplation, and began to harness the incredible power of imagination.

I delved into a vivid mental scenario of what my life would be like if I placed the building on the market. In this imaginative act, I conversed with my real estate agent, and in my mind's eye, I heard her say, "This is the quickest listing I've ever sold." My inner conversation continued as I posed questions and obtained the responses I needed. I envisioned our discussion as I pushed her to provide the words I longed to hear.

When we eventually listed the property, a mere seven days passed before an offer materialized. Not only did it meet our asking price, but it exceeded it. This was precisely what

I had imagined – a swift sale with my agent declaring it as one of her most rapid and successful listings.

My secret lay in unwavering faith in my imaginal act. I committed to this daily practice until I felt it was a certainty. And when, after seven days, my agent uttered those very words, it was a testimony to the power of imagination and the unwavering faith that fuels it. You see, your imagination is the architect of your reality. The key isn't just imagining; it's having faith in your imagination. My focus wasn't on the visual details; it was on the words and the conversation, and that made all the difference.

I share this testimony to underscore the transformative potential of controlling your inner conversations. What you think, what you meditate upon, and the conversations you hold within yourself—they have the power to shape your future. Change your life by gaining mastery over the thoughts and inner dialogues you entertain. Create the reality you desire by thinking from it, by making your conversations a reflection of the life you wish to live.

The essence of it all is faith in your imaginal act. It's more than just imagining; it's believing in the power of your imagination to shape your future. Your inner conversations are the architects of your destiny. Embrace this truth, and you'll unlock the extraordinary potential within you.

www.ingramcontent.com/pod-product-compliance
Lightning Source LLC
Chambersburg PA
CBHW031432130726
47989CB00003B/1106